How to Get Away With Money

A Guide to personal investing, the foundation to taking control of your investing life, and insiders look to the brokers that get away with your money.

Donald Draper

Introduction

Andrew Carnegie once said as I grow older I pay less attention to what men say, I just watch what they do. This world is full of men that create companies that say a lot of things and make a lot of promises but never come through. Specifically financial advisors and the brokerages they work for.

I am an average person, just like you, that does not have hundred of thousands of dollars stashed away for retirement. Neither do I have the time during the day to trade stocks and attempt to beat the market. I am not an expert on volatility or standard deviation or any other mathematical terms used to confuse the average investor into making a bad

Donald Draper

decision. But what I do have is the experience that comes from working with thousands of investors and seeing that most of them are all in the same boat. They do not know what they are doing with their investments. It is not from a lack of wanting and many times it is not from a lack of trying. Most of the time it boils down to people not having the right education to accurately make their own financial decisions. In my experiences, I have seen time and time again people make ridiculous financial decisions either because a friend told them to or because some cut-rate financial advisor told them to.

    There used to be a time when people didn't have to worry about making financial decisions on their own. The company they worked for would take care of them. A person worked at a place for forty plus years and when they hit retirement, waiting for them was a pension that paid them a reasonable amount of money every month until they died. On top of that was the supplement of social security to add even more income. Sounds like a pretty worry free situation. But sadly those days are gone.

    In present day if you want to make it and not work your entire life you must know how to make money yourself. One option is you can stuff a ton of your money into your 401k plan at work, if your job offers one, and then pray that it doesn't disappear on any given horrible day in the market. Not to mention your 401k plan limits you to the

Donald Draper

favorable mix that your plan administrator selects. Oh and that plan administrator probably doesn't know any more about the market than you do. They are just choosing option that makes the most
business sense.

    You could also go rogue and attempt to grow your funds yourself. But where do you start there? Either you pay a financial advisor to watch your money and check on you once a year, fingers crossed if he even does that, or you can read a couple of articles and watch MSNBC while trying to figure out a craft that people get multiple licenses and certifications in to get a handle on.

    What regular person has the time or money for all of that? The truth is even if you

Donald Draper

wanted to pay someone to manage your money what are they really doing?

This book will help you understand personal investing in three parts while helping you take control of your future. At the very least you will know how to make good choices with your investments. Part One is going to educate you on what most "financial advisors" do. Not the financial advisors who work for multimillion dollar clients. No those individuals actually do some resemblance to work. The financial advisors we will discuss check on your account once a year or answer a call when you dial a 1-800 number, the biggest sham in the world in my opinion. Part Two is going to educate you on the basics of personal investing. This will help give you the same

Donald Draper

basic knowledge that the financial advisors in Part One, who make close to six figures off of your money, apply. Part Three is going to actually educate you on how to apply these principles in your own life so you can go out there and select a reputable brokerage, open the right accounts, and manage your money yourself.

    No one teaches the average person these things for reasons that I don't know beside the fact that they want to get away with your money. The truth is financial stability is available to everyone as long as you have some basic knowledge of investing and are open to doing a little bit of your own research. There are products and strategies out there that help ensure this. But it is not easy and

Donald Draper

there is no silver bullet.

    This book will not make you a millionaire in three months or setup any crazy pipe dreams. The first step in this process of investing for yourself is saving money, which some people do not want to do and that is ok. If you don't think you are capable of saving this book isn't for you. But if you believe in your future and are willing to develop the discipline to save for it then you can apply the principals in this book and set yourself up for a brighter financial future.

Donald Draper

How to Get Away With Money   10

Donald Draper

Part I

Chapter 1
How Does This All Work?

As a former licensed financial advisor, I have seen the other side of personal investing industry that the normal consumer is not exposed to. What you read in the book will shock you.

With simple knowledge, you can master your own finances and feel confident that your financial future is on track. Before writing this book I was personally tired of telling different people the same things over and over again. What should be common knowledge seemed like foreign languages to most of the people I

Donald Draper

interacted with. The motivation behind this book was my frustration with the personal investing industry. How can people be so clueless with the most important aspect of their lives? I asked this question over and over again. What I failed to realize is that if all the people I came into contact with knew what they were doing I wouldn't have a job. There was inventive to keeping people dumb.

I was formerly an advisor, investment consultant, financial representative all several different names for a person who just has a securities license but really doesn't do anything with it. (For the rest of this book I will be referring to these individuals as advisors.) I was able to see behind the scenes of multiple full-service brokerages. From this experience, I

Donald Draper

was exposed to common practices that were the same no matter where I worked, from well established American institutions that have been around for a hundred years to several small level startups. The common theme all these companies have is that they are huge money printers.

One thing to keep in mind is everything is a business. The best, most charitable companies in the world still exist to make money. But there comes a point where making money becomes the only objective. These institutions are guilty of only caring about growing money. No matter what sales gimmick you hear every single person that comes into contact with an employee of one of these institutions only has one objective and that is

Donald Draper

to sell you something. Anytime you hear someone say "we are not trying to sell you something", they are selling you something. I dare you to call one of these companies and say you want to open an account but do not want to be sold anything. You will be met with a reply that we aren't trying to sell you anything, sir/ma'am. Bull Shit!

    The new buzz word strategy for these firms is "service to sales" and they all teach it to their employees. Brokerage firms and banks are the kings of service to sales. What this boils down to is that you the customer can't live without interacting with one of these establishments. These companies do not have to do much selling to hook you in. And once they have you it becomes a near impossible

Donald Draper

task to leave.

Why is this important? Well, it's because these companies live off of bringing in more and more money. They will draw you in with low trading fees or free accounts, but in reality, they do more stuff in a day to make more money off your money than you could even imagine. They don't charge you upfront fees in the beginning because the possession of your money makes them billions on billions of dollars. We won't go into details on how exactly they make money but the important thing to remember is that they are getting something from you from the start. Why do they have to get more of your money?

Why do they try to assess your needs and ask you a lot of questions when you just

Donald Draper

need a password reset on their website or need a distribution check? The reason is the billions they already make off of you are not enough. Every year quotas and goals get higher and higher, their shareholders/ owners want to see more growth and the companies have to figure out ways to pump consumers out of more money.

That is was why "service to sales" was invented. The brokerages needed a way to make more money but at the same time not seem like pushy car salesmen. (In my opinion, I respect the pushy car salesman more. At least we can clearly see that he is trying to fool you out of your money.) These "customer service reps or customer advocates" are disguised as friendly people who claim to care

Donald Draper

about your needs. And I am sure some of them do legitimately care about their customers but in reality, most of them don't care at all. The customer is just another hurdle to increasing their bonuses at the end of the quarter. I have nothing against sales people at all, but when they sell people things they do not need or take advantage of unsuspecting people I have a problem.

The common principle in this "service to sales" method is taking your stated need, a distribution check for example, and morphing that conversation by asking you enough questions so you start to feel so bad about yourself and your current situation (they call this an emotional driver) that you agree that you have no clue what you're doing with your

Donald Draper

finances. Once you agree with them they have you in their pocket, and you will agree to whatever they prescribe you need.

In all reality, this way of selling is great and can help people who do not realize that they need help get the assistance with what they need. But remember what I said earlier these individuals do not care about your needs they are just trying to make a sell.

I was one of these customer service guys pretending to care about the customer just like everyone else. Behind the scenes, though I was all about the sell and getting higher numbers than anyone else. After years of this mentality, I now see the faults of this mindset and realize that being a salesman was not why I entered this industry. I really and truly

Donald Draper

wanted to help people but what I was doing was just selling things that people shouldn't need or at least need to pay for.

Donald Draper

How to Get Away With Money　　　　　　　　　　　　　　20

Donald Draper

Chapter 2
What are you paying for?

Now that you know how you are set up for the sale you can now learn what they are selling you. Most brokerage firms fall into three categories: Self-managed or directed, fully managed, or a hybrid offering both options. The difference boils down to if you think you can manage your money yourself or if you want someone else to do it for you. The first type that we will discuss is the one that is the biggest rip off for normal people, fully managed.

Fully managed firms consist of assigning a financial advisor to you that supposedly manages your money. Many times they pitch that they have fully licensed advisors (series 7 and series 66 or the 63 and 65 combinations) and have a CFP designation. (CFP, certified financial planner). You probably have no idea what any of that means but it sounds fancy. That is the point and exactly where the deception starts. Do not get me wrong those licenses and designations require work and dedication to get but anyone with the right motivation can get them. The kicker is most of the material covered in these licensing examines most advisors barely use and just forget after the test. They are no different than your average college graduate who forgot what they learned in their core classes because they will never use the information.

Advisors are required to have those licenses so you as the consumer can assume

Donald Draper

and feel like you are dealing with safe, reputable people. In reality, they do not get approval from FINRA, the SEC, or any organization. They basically just file that they are who they say they are and have passed a couple of tests. I say this because I want you to understand that they are not any more capable of doing for you what you cannot do for yourself. They are not doctors or rocket scientists.

These advisors are pitched as individuals that can manage your money for you and get you on a track to financial freedom. In a sense, they do manage the account by putting your information into some planning software that claims to run simulations based on your suitability, risk tolerance, income, etc. to spit out some investing strategy that is custom to you. The truth is if you are an average person, with two hundred and fifty thousand dollars to invest and below, these systems only give two basic management options. The two options are a growth portfolio or a conservative one. If you are an older client you may get growth with income but this is a rarity. You are not really paying for a person to manage your account but really paying for a person to ask you questions for an hour and then put that into a computer to get one of three options.

Picture this, an affordable advisor charges around one percent. On a hundred thousand dollar account you would be paying a thousand dollars a year for someone to ask questions and then put the answers into a computer program. For the financial advisor, this is not a bad way to make a solid living and why so many people picture financial advisors driving around in Porsches. They are really just focused on bringing people in and putting their money into these managed programs. The art of the profession is not actually planning for the customer but selling them on bringing their money in. The firm also gets their cut as well to make money off your money.

The rebuttal to this is, yes I am paying a thousand dollars a year to have my account managed but at least I do not have to worry about it and I get solid performance that I wouldn't otherwise get. Or at least I have a person I can call when I have questions and need talking off a ledge when things go crazy

Donald Draper

in the market. These are two great points and responses to rejection that all advisors use in their sales pitches when a customer questions their worth. But when you take a deeper look you will see that an advisor is not worth anywhere near a thousand dollars.

We will cover the market and patterns of the market in Part 2 but for now, let's discuss the performance factor for a second. The performance of these so called fully managed accounts is comparable to most robot funds (mutual funds run by an algorithm that adjusts the asset mix for you) and target date funds (mutual funds run by a fund manager who adjusts the asset mix over time according to an investor's age). The thing about these two fund options is that you can buy them yourself for less than one percent in fees. That's right, you can get the same performance yourself that you're paying a so-called advisor for cheaper yourself.

Most advisors do nothing. He or she doesn't pick any investments, doesn't have access to anything that you don't have access to yourself, and barely knows any more than you do. As a former advisor, it took me quitting to realize no one ever taught me anything about the very things we were selling. I couldn't tell you anything about funds or products, why you are buying them. I just trusted the companies I worked for. The only thing I had to know how to do was sell. My job didn't revolve around knowing, it was about bringing more people and more money into the

Donald Draper

firm. That doesn't seem very beneficial and in the client's best interest now does it?

If you do not get anything from reading this book, just remember if you choose to work with an advisor ask them these three questions: What do you do? What is the performance? Why do I pay you? I guarantee they'll throw some garbage value proposition about taking control of your money for you blah blah blah or having the knowledge of knowing when to pull out of the market. They are basically saying that you are an idiot and aren't capable of making unemotional decisions. And of course you aren't, unemotional decisions are only easy to make when the consequences don't affect you but you're not an idiot you are just misinformed.

Donald Draper

Chapter 3
Can you handle all this?

So far we have covered fully managed firms where you give some guy who studied for a test once and forget all that knowledge, control of the most important thing in your life. And most people would have read Chapter 2 and said I don't have an advisor, I manage my money myself. True most people who are the average investor go at it alone and this is also costly.

In Part 2 we will cover the basics of investing so that you can become a better, more educated investor, but we need to cover some of the major mistakes that I have seen all self-directed investors make that self-directed brokerages love. Remember these companies make money by selling people things, and they can't sell a self-directed person much. So they capitalize on the common mistakes these investors makes.

    Mistake number one that the self-directed investor makes is that they do not educate themselves on the basics of the market. The stock market is a game, just like Vegas with flashing lights and all. Would you walk up to a poker table without learning the game? No. But people open brokerage accounts and IRAs like free gifts and just start gambling away their savings. Why I have no idea. I was fully licensed for years before I got the confidence to trade my money on my own. But somehow every day people step right up

Donald Draper

and they lose time and time again. Do your own research, find out what you like and what works for you if you want to manage your own investments. I will say this over and over again, do your own research and find out what truly works for you. Just because your uncle, doctor, or boyfriend says something is a buy does not make it a buy. More times than not he or she is just as clueless as you are to what they are buying and probably got that idea from someone who was also clueless. Individuals get rare certifications, licenses, and degrees to master the market, your cousin that sells mortgages does not. The stock market is not an easy game that you can just jump into. You need some education and skill to play and make a profit. (Part 2 will be your crash course on education and skill) Off the back, the cards are stacked against you and the self-directed brokerage takes advantage of that.

The mistakes made by the uneducated investor are profitable to the self-directed brokerage. Uneducated investors are more likely to trade a lot more often than the patient educated investors. This brings in substantially more money for brokerage firms in terms of commissions (the fee you pay when you buy or sell a stock). Uneducated investors also tend to use tools they have no business usually without the proper education, like margin (taking out loans against their assets) and options (contracts to buy stocks at a certain price in the future). Using these tools can cause an investor to fall into debt.

Donald Draper

Purely self-directed brokerages rarely exist anymore because, with service to sales, uneducated investors present an amazing sales opportunity. With more and more people going at it themselves you see more people feeling unsure about their investments and failing. They aren't educated, they are going off of hunches from their friends, and they are gullible. Perfect sales opportunities. When you are lost and someone tells you that they can get you on the right track you will listen. And that is all they need to do.

With these new sales opportunities, the self-directed brokerages have realized that they are sitting on countless sales leads. The customer bases are filled with people who are

Donald Draper

trying to manage their money themselves and are failing. Many are losing money, making money but have unrealistic expectations of the market, or some just never do anything with the money.

So with this golden opportunity sitting in their laps, the self-directed firms hired a bunch of "customer service reps" that are really licensed salespeople (and in many cases former advisors or people didn't make it as advisors) who are incentivized to make customers feel like they can't handle their own money. This scenario is exactly why service to sales was invented. The goal is to set the customer up during a regular interaction to reveal to them that they are not in the position to manage their own investments. Maybe

Donald Draper

these customer service representatives question your strategy, which a lot of times you don't have because no one tells you that you need one, or they ask you if you have the time to research and manage your money, because investments move all the time and if you miss a day you will miss everything. Do not get me wrong, these are all valid points that I totally agree with. But these individuals do not help you like they should or could because that wouldn't make them money. Helping people fairly doesn't drive sales goals or bring in money.

These service reps either sell you a product that most likely is more expensive than what you could get yourself and then they convince you to bring in more money or they bounce you off to an advisor who does that on their end. This leads to big bonuses where customer service reps make six figures. Not bad for someone taking thirty phone calls a day and not working to bring in a single client.

In my opinion, these people are the worst, and I was one of them at one point and enjoyed it. Until one day I left a good firm for more money had my eyes opened. I worked for possibly the worst firm in the country. I stood by and watched as many average investors were either being taken advantage or allowed to make stupid, costly decisions. These firms and their employees pretend to help people but are really motivated by making money and tons of it.

After years of being apart of this system,

Donald Draper

I had an idea to stop the cycle of people taking advantage of and decided to write this book. I have spoken with thousands of people who have said to me over and over again that in a ten-minute conversation with me they learned more than they had learned in their lives. Motivated by this I want to pass on the knowledge that I have to help people not avoid getting taken advantage of by people who are just seeing them as a number on a bonus check. I wanted to share the knowledge that I have to hopefully provide you with the education and know how to hopefully manage your investment the right way yourself.

Donald Draper

How to Get Away With Money   38

Donald Draper

Part 2

Chapter 4
What are all these things?

Part 2 is all about the basics of personal investing. Many of the people I have interacted with other the years struggle with the basic concepts of investing. Without a proper education on the basics, people somehow think that they can go out and invest. This is not only erroneous thinking but also what I believe is thinking that is encouraged by the market and companies that sell securities. An unbelievable amount of mistakes that are made can be avoided by basic knowledge of

Donald Draper

the game of investing.

The place where we will start accounts. The very first question of investing is what are you investing for? The answer to this question determines where money needs to be in order to take advantage of the various rules and regulations around these accounts. Too many people answer the question, Why do you want to invest, with one answer, to make money. There is nothing wrong with that answer but it is not the right answer. There always has to be a legitimate, tangible reason for why you want to invest. This is so that you can have an obtainable goal to strive for. Whether it is retirement, providing a college education for your children, or saving for a car; you have to have a hard number to strive for. The stock market is not a place where dreams come true like Disney World, it is a tool that supplements hard work to accomplish a task, like a construction site. If you remember this concept it will help you not get ripped off by brokerage companies and put your investment goals in perspective.

You already know who the people that make the most money for brokerages are, the people who make horrible decisions trying to chase a number that doesn't exist time and time again. These individuals are caught in a cycle of winning a little bit and losing a lot. They do it over and over again like a gambler because they are focused on the short term. We will cover this more in Part 3.

The basic accounts are regular brokerage

Donald Draper

accounts and IRAs. Basic accounts are pretty easy to understand. They are accounts where you can buy and sell stocks, bonds, and ETFs. You have your standard Individual account with just one owner and then you have joint accounts with multiple owners. When considering these basics accounts one thing to always keep in mind is to open one up at a firm that has "transfer on death" options. When working with all money, not just investments, you need to always know what will happen to the funds in the event of your passing. Probate court is expensive and a pain for your loved ones to go through. Make it easy on them and name who you want in the beginning.

    IRAs are another different animal. For

reasons unknown to me, it is not mandatory to teach people what IRAs are in school. IRA stands for Individual Retirement Account and these accounts by far are the most important to a person's financial well-being. They were created specifically for retirement purposes so that investors could realize tax-advantaged growth. IRAs also have a contribution limits of fifty-five hundred a year if you are under fifty and sixty-five hundred if you are over fifty. Contributions can only be made when you earn income. There are two types of basic IRAs, Roth and Traditional. The more common is a traditional IRA because they have been around longer than the Roth and they are geared more toward the common investor. Traditional IRAs are funded with pretax money. This means that contributions to the traditional IRAs are considered tax deductible or they come from money that was deducted from wages before the taxes were taken out. The main reason to use a traditional IRAs is to stash money away tax deferred until retirement when you are most likely are earning less money and the tax burden is lessened. Keep in mind you have to stop contributing to a traditional IRA when you are seventy and a half years old, where the IRS requires you to take minimum required distributions.

    The Roth IRA is the exact opposite. People pay taxes upfront on their contributions and then take the gains and the principal out tax-free. The best way to choose which one is the right choice for you is to consider your tax

Donald Draper

situation now and what you expect your tax situation to be in the future. In my experience, most people will do just fine with a traditional IRA. Most normal people will make less money in retirement than in their working years. One last thing on IRAs is that there are early withdraw penalties for distributions before the age of fifty-nine.

    401ks, 403bs, 401A, Simples, Self-employed 401ks, and 457s are all employee plans that we will cover briefly. These plans are offered through employers (or brokerage firms that offer products for self-employed individuals) and give you the ability to contribute more toward your retirement than IRAs. But the downside of these plans is that you are limited in your

Donald Draper

investments options.

The last common account type that is a popular choice for the average investor are educational accounts. There are two types of educational accounts 529s and ESAs (educational savings accounts). 529s have a higher contribution limit than ESA, $14,000 a year as opposed to $2000. I suggest 529 plans because of the higher contribution limits and the investment choices within the plan. They are similar to 401k plans in that you are limited in your investment choices. 529 plans run by states and are made up by investments chosen by the states. The investment mix is a little on the conservative side but you do not want a ton of risk with your children's education. You would just want steady growth through the years.

Donald Draper

How to Get Away With Money 48

Donald Draper

Chapter 5
Stocks, Bonds, Mutual Funds, and ETFs?

Now that we have covered the different types of accounts we must now cover the securities within these accounts. Too many times in my career I witnessed people opening accounts and wanting to invest without knowing exactly what they are attempting to invest in. You wouldn't try to play football without knowing the positions so why would you try to invest without knowing what you're going to invest in?

First, we will cover stocks, the most common investment there is. Stocks represent an ownership stake in a company broken up into shares. These shares have rights as a shareholder of the company that we will not get into here because the average investor does not concern themselves with these things. The important thing to investors is how they make money off of stocks. These investments trade based off of price fluctuations. Meaning that you buy the stock at one price and sell at another. The price of a stock can fluctuate for multiple reasons but the main one is supply and demand. Supply and demand are a strong force on the stocks that motivates many uneducated investors. In Part 3 we will cover the proper strategy for picking stocks but for now just keep in mind how stocks are traded. Remember when dealing with stocks they have the potential to lose all of their value. A Company's' stock can lose value for multiple reasons from a bankruptcy to people simply not being interested in the stock anymore.

Next up are bonds. Bonds differ from stocks in that they are not an ownership stake in a company but rather a loan of to the company. You give the company money, in many instances in thousand dollar increments, and the company promises to give you the money back as well as interest. In many cases, the principal is guaranteed as well as the interest but with some companies, it is not. Bonds generally have a smaller upside than stocks but they are less risky. Their value revolves around interest rates that are influenced by the government.

Donald Draper

Bonds tend to be used by older investors that appreciate the safety and do not have a need for impressive growth. With that being said, bonds are needed for a well-rounded portfolio to achieve proper diversification. In Part 3 we will cover these two topics in more detail.

The next investment vehicle is mutual funds. Mutual funds are defined as bundles of securities packaged and sold together in order to lower market risk through diversification. When you package multiple securities together your risk exposure decreases significantly because you will not have to live and die by what one security does. If one security loses value another security can lighten the blow. Mutual funds can be made up by multiple stocks, bonds, or other mutual funds for exponentially more diversification. With the lowered risk you should keep in mind that there will be lower growth. Mutual funds are not perfect and do have some risk but for long term steady growth they cannot be beaten. If you are willing to take on more risk than the average mutual fund there are specialized funds that carry more risk. The choice of mutual fund really comes down to your investment objective. Do you want steady growth or do you think you can get capital appreciation? Although mutual funds are popular many people do not understand how they produce gains for the customer. Investing in mutual funds is like investing in a company directly. As the fund gains in value, your

Donald Draper

investment gains in value. You can also gain income from dividends and capital gains (the gains from the selling of securities within the fund).

The last securities we will cover is ETFs or Exchange Traded Funds. These securities are relatively new and are a hybrid of stocks and mutual funds. They are made up of many different securities like mutual funds but they trade on exchanges. The investor makes money when they sell the ETF for a higher price than when they bought it just for a stock. Since they are made up of different securities you can also see dividends and capital gains as income in these securities.

There are many more securities out there for more sophisticated investors but for our purposes, as basic investors, you only need to know stocks, bonds, ETFs, and mutual funds.

Donald Draper

How to Get Away With Money 56

Donald Draper

Chapter 6

Where can I open an account?

Now that you have gained a basic understanding of accounts and securities you must now know where to acquire them. As we discussed in Part 1 there are different types of investment firms out there (self-directed, fully managed, or a hybrid) and you must choose where to want to do your business.

Over my years of experience and working for many different firms I have seen the many different options out there. Some firms are great for the average investor and others, not so much. Every firm is a little different but there are some major characteristics that you need to look for in a firm to ensure that it will be the right fit for you.

First, free accounts and low trading fees. The major reason that I wrote this book was to save regular investors money and empower them to take over their own investments. If a firm charges you for an account or has traded over ten dollars then you are getting robbed. Most self-directed firms will meet these expectations but fully managed firms will not. The main complaint with fully managed firms is that they will fee the hell out of you. I have seen investors being charged upwards of forty dollars for trades. The firms that charge these fees will most likely also have a yearly maintenance fee for their accounts. With fully managed firms not only are you paying a fee for a worthless advisor, you will most likely be nickel and dimed in fees. The main point of this book is to minimize your costs and get rid of financial advisors. Just avoid fully managed firms.

Second, you need to find a firm that offers the securities you need to setup a proper portfolio. In Part 3 I will show you exactly what this looks like, but know it consists of stocks, bonds, ETFs, and mutual funds. If you ever run into a firm that does not offer ETFs, mutual funds, or bonds they most likely are trying to attract "starter" investors. They call them starter investors but in reality, they are just uneducated investors. These are the people that believe that they can get in on a penny

Donald Draper

stock that may jump to twenty dollars a share and make them rich. These types of investors might as well be gamblers. They may hit it big once but they will lose more often than not. The firms that cater to these people are basically casinos.

Third, chose a firm that offers accounts with a transfer on death capabilities or beneficiaries. I do not know of many firms that do not offer this but the last firm I worked for didn't. Asset transfer should be the biggest concern around an investment account right next to what investment strategy you choose. Investment accounts are different from checking accounts. They are vehicles for asset appreciation over time. The goal around your investments should be a long term goal, and

Donald Draper

although we may not like talking about it some people never make it to their long term goals due to life coming to an unexpected end. Chances are that even if you do not pass unexpectedly if you are a savvy, smart investor (my goal for you and hopefully your goal) you will pass on with assets left over for your loved ones. I said this earlier but the probate process is a pain for your love ones. Do the right thing and name a beneficiary. You will always have the ability to change them if other life events happen. Do not open an account at a firm that does not have that capability. They are not serious about you as a long term customer and you shouldn't let them take you for granted. There is no logical excuse for it and there are so many firms out

Donald Draper

there that make this process easy and convenient for you.

Four also goes back to the last firm that I worked at. You should pick a firm that allows you easy access to your funds. Whether you want to take a withdraw or transfer money to another account, if they want a form signed and mailed/faxed in or you need a notary stamp, do not open an account there. No matter what excuse they use it should never be a pain or a stressful event to get access to your money. With investing there are rules that are in place that can hold up funds like settlement periods (settlement periods are the time it takes after the purchase or sale of a security, three days for stock, ETFs and one day for mutual fund) but if it takes a week and some paperwork to get your funds, that is not an appropriate firm.

Lastly, choose a firm that offers free investment planning software. In Part 1 we discussed what exactly your run of the mill financial advisor does. Basically, you're paying them one percent or more of your money to ask you questions and put them into a program once a year. Well, most respectable firms have a just as good version of that software available to the public. It is not as in depth as what the advisors use but it is more than good enough to get the job done. All of the large firms that you should be working with offer this but the smaller ones do not. This is for obvious reasons, they need customers to opt into working with their advisors to bring in more money. With what you have learned in Part 1 and 2 as well as what you will learn in Part 3 you will be able to use this planning software appropriately and not need some overpaid data collector to do it for you.

Now that you have basic knowledge on accounts, the securities within these accounts, and what to consider when opening these accounts; you can now take a deeper dive and learn how to apply these principles to your own finances and take control of your financial life.

Donald Draper

Part 3

Chapter 7

What is the starting point?

If you are reading this book most likely you are a novice investor with some or no money saved up, but you are motivated to get yourself on track. You now understand that the investing industry is a tough place to navigate on your own but with a little guidance, you have all the tools you need to be successful.

Now you will not be perfect at managing your investments right away. It takes patience and learning from your mistakes to get it right. But once you do master your own investments

Donald Draper

you will feel great about your position and avoid wasting money on fees and needless mistakes.

Knowing all of this it is time to actually begin investing. Anytime you invest you have to keep in mind that money doesn't have an end. In my past when I asked people why they wanted to invest they would always respond the same exact way from my father to complete strangers. Everyone would say "I want to make money". And I would respond "what do you mean?" This would start a back and forth conversation that would eventually lead to that person telling me a goal. Making money is great but without a goal, you have no clue how much is enough. If you don't know how much is enough then no amount of money

Donald Draper

will satisfy you and you will develop unrealistic expectations. With investing, unrealistic expectations can lead to making awful realistic investment choices that cause you to go broker overnight.

The first thing to do when you make the decision to invest is come up with the goal for your investment. This will take your dream out of the clouds and make it a reality. Whether you want to save for retirement, plan for your children's college, or make an emergency fund a goal must be established.

Once your goal is established you must then come up with a number that would make your goal a reality. The number gives you something to shoot for. This number should

Donald Draper

never be something unrealistic and must be obtainable. Chances are if you only have a hundred dollars to invest you won't turn that into a million dollars.

After your number is established you must come up with a time frame. A time frame gives you an idea of what you have to do and risks you have to be comfortable to take in order to make your goal happen. A time frame also further solidifies the goal. The goal becomes even more real when the clock is ticking. Just like your number you selected, the time has to also be realistic. Unless you are extremely lucky you are most likely not going to make a million dollars in a year. I do not care what your friend of a friend said they did

Donald Draper

one time a few years ago.

Let me remind you that if you are reading this book you need to be investing for the right reasons. You should always be focused on making responsible investing decisions for your future. Being realistic is the key to everything. The brokerages that we covered in Part 1 make billions and billions of dollars off of the fools that believe investing is like playing the lottery.

Now that you have developed your goal, your number, and your time you must develop your risk tolerance. Risk tolerance is the amount of risk you are willing to take to accomplish your goal. Many companies and their asset allocation software will suggest a risk tolerance based on your age, but I have found that this really puts people into a box. Everyone is different and everyone's goals are different so I believe it is up to the person to define their own risk tolerance based on their goal. Many people feel like investing is super risky and that people never do well with it but those individuals are just afraid of what they do not understand. You, on the other hand, have a proper understanding of the stock market. The next thing you need is a proper understanding of risk. The risk is the odds that you will lose your money. The tricky thing about risk is that when it is persona risk it can not be quantified. There are ways to measure risk in securities but the personal risk is a feeling that you feel in order to make your goal

Donald Draper

happen.

Since personal risk is hard to quantify you have to imagine it on a scale of one to ten. One consisting of very conservative securities like bonds or certificates of deposits to ten being penny stocks. The middle would be a good fifty-fifty mix of stocks and bonds. This mix gives you a good range of securities you should consider investing in for your goal. For review, bonds and certificates of deposit are interest bearing securities with guaranteed principal. Penny stocks are stocks that are not traded on the major exchanges, made up of companies that are not well established, and tend to go bankrupt or never grow. Penny stocks are highly risky, some firms don't even hold them, and more often than not never make investors money. This is not to say people have never gotten rich or made money off them, it is possible but not likely.

With most goals, you want to be responsible and make the right investment decisions by selecting a risk tolerance more toward the middle of the scale. This is why time and the number you select are of such high importance. With a small number to start, say a hundred dollars, a goal of thousand dollars, and a long time frame of ten years you can take a less risk because your goal is more obtainable. Making thousand dollars in ten years on one hundred dollars is ten percent growth each year without compounding. The stock market as whole averages eight percent growth each year for comparison. The whole market is heavily diversified and falls at about a high five on the risk scale for perspective.

Take that same equation and shorten the time or increase the number then you would have to take more risk and end up at a six or seven on the scale. A six or a seven would make for a riskier stock position. Always remember the more risk the more reward but also the higher possibility you could lose your money.

It is the exact opposite for the reverse if you decreased the number or increased the time you can take less risk. You would most likely land on the four or three side of the scale. On this end, you would be looking at a bond fund (mutual fund made up of bonds) or an allocation that is more bond leaning.

Now that we have covered risk and you have an idea of where you are going, we are going to cover how you select the investments that will work for you.

Donald Draper

Chapter 8
What are you going to pick?

I will be honest right now, the way I was trained and brought up as an advisor I tend to be a little more conservative than most. I strongly believe that mutual funds are the way to go for the average investor but one size fits all investing does not work for everyone. With that said, you have to find it in yourself to make a decision on how much of your personal time you want to devote to your investments.

A huge selling point on working with an advisor that many brokerages use to lure in investors is the problem of the time needed to manage your own investments. Time is money though and we are talking about your money

Donald Draper

and your time. If time is a major concern then you should consider the more conservative route consisting of mutual funds. These securities tend to be diversified and managed by a fund manager. Mutual funds make solid long-term investments but they are not without risks.

If you do have time to really devote to your investing or maybe your goal requires you to take on more risk, you should consider ETFs or a good mix of stocks. If you choose this route you should be checking your investments at least once a day to make sure nothing is tanking to the point where it won't bring itself back up. You should also be monitoring for the opposite thing happening. When a stock takes off you need to closely monitor it to know

Donald Draper

when to sell. The time you have to devote to investing is key to how you are going to select your investments.

The other key is asset allocation. Just like with risk I view asset allocation a little differently than most brokerage firms do. In my career, I have seen firms use asset allocation to define investors. Many cut-rate, generic advisors are taught as a rule of thumb investors should subtract their age from one hundred to calculate the percentage of equities in their portfolio. This works great if your goal is retirement but not all people are investing for retirement. Just like the risk, I believe asset allocation should revolve around your goal and not your age.

Donald Draper

I have said many times you are now a responsible investor. Now you are educated on how this game works, your risk tolerance falls between a three and seven, and you understand diversification is key to minimizing losses. The last thing you have to cover is asset allocation. Asset allocation is the percentage mix of equity (stocks), debt (bonds), and sometimes cash in a portfolio. The more conservative you are the more your allocation will lean toward debt and the riskier you are the more equities. Cash is money you have available at a moments notice for emergencies. I am not a supporter of having a money in cash in a brokerage account. That is what savings accounts at banks are for. If you are going to invest then invest.

Donald Draper

Asset allocation will play a key role in the securities you select. Whether you are going to go for mutual funds or stocks with a few bond options.

One last thing, when you start investing you need to shape your investments to the amount of money you have. It is a sad reality but in investing the smaller the amount of money you have the smaller the selection of investments available to you. Everyone has to start somewhere but where you start really affects your risk because of the securities available to you may have more risk. For example, most mutual funds have a minimum investment of two thousand five hundred

Donald Draper

dollars. Bonds have a minimum investment of a thousand. Good blue chip stocks are trading in the hundreds.

If you don't have at least two thousand five hundred dollars to invest I would suggest saving up in a checking or savings account until you have that much to invest. Or you could use that money for educational purposes. Depending on your goal and your time you may have a golden opportunity to play with some stocks and see what you like. Buy a few stocks that are lower values, avoid penny stocks, please. This attempt and failure process will give you a better idea of what works and what doesn't for you. It is a great learning opportunity that many people are not exposed to. Many people do not get serious

Donald Draper

about investing until it is too late in their lives. Once again, though, if you have a time-sensitive goal do not experiment, save and then get on track.

Hopefully, you have the two thousand five hundred dollars or more available to start, and you can learn how to appropriately select the right investments for your goal. I want to stress if you do not you can definitely continue reading the book but these principals will not apply to you.

Donald Draper

How to Get Away With Money

Donald Draper

Chapter 9

Are you ready to begin?

You are finally ready to pick out investments on your own investments. Like we covered in chapter 8, the smaller the amount of money available to invest the more limited the securities available. But time frame is the most important factor here. The shorter the amount of time for your goal the more risk you tend to have to take to accomplish your goal.

No matter where you start in terms of money available to invest, diversification is key. You want to have a diversified portfolio. There is no one solution for investing no matter what some fund manager or advisor says. You must have a healthy mix securities

Donald Draper

to accomplish your goals.

    For a goal where you have a short time frame to start off (five years or less), you should consider a good mix of ETFs. ETFs, as you, know offer a good amount of diversification at an affordable price. But with diversification, you are lowering risk and could lower the reward. So that is one important factor to keep in mind. If ETFs are too safe for you than I would suggest a good mix of blue chip, large cap stocks, (established companies with high market capitalization in the tens of billions) and some riskier mid-cap stocks. Remember picking your own stocks could have more reward than ETFs but you will be talking your diversification and asset allocation

Donald Draper

yourself.

But for a goal with a longer time frame, ETFs and single stocks just won't work unless you want to constantly trade things in and out of your portfolio. There also needs to be more time involved to manage the account. The king of long term investments is mutual funds. Most of the time these funds have a long-term investment objective, to begin with. The funds are made to last over a long period of time and offer great diversification. There are also mutual funds out there that are made up of just bonds which work for an investor that wants to be more conservative.

There comes a time though when time frame doesn't matter much and a goal disappears. This tends to happen at the end of one's life when they do not have any particular goal or cause to leave their money to. This is also the case when someone has a large amount of money and really no desire to truly invest for a goal. This rarely happens but I did see it from time to time. For situations like this bonds or certificates of deposit can play a large role in your investment strategy. With these guaranteed securities that barely interest you as an investor need to consider inflation. Inflation is the rate that the value of money naturally shrinks over time. Inflation on average is about three percent. With these interest bearing products, you need to have a rate that at least beats inflation or will be losing value in your money.

Donald Draper

Chapter 10

How are going you pick them?

Now that you have an idea of what to pick you we are going to cover how to actually pick these investments. Many people tend to pick investments just because they know a name or they heard from someone that this was a good investment. Good investing requires research. Even after reading this book you aren't fully ready to invest. Research is needed to make an educated decision.

We will start with picking stocks. Picking stocks can seem to be overwhelming at first but with a solid strategy, it will be easy. There are millions of them out there in different sectors and in different parts of the world.

Donald Draper

Picking the right ones can seem like a daunting task with no place to start. But you already should have an idea of where to start. Since you are now an educated investor you know that for serious goals penny stocks are a not an option. With concrete achievable goals, you will only be looking at a relatively small number of stocks. Most of the stocks you should be looking into should be from established companies with a solid track record of growth, profits, and maybe dividend payouts. The stocks you pick must also fall in line with your risk tolerance and time frame. Most blue chip stocks grow steady but may not grow at a rate that is consistent with your goals. Research is key to finding stocks in sectors that are growing.

Donald Draper

Most individuals can not comprehend that even when the market is declining there are stocks that are growing. The Nasdaq, S&P 500, and Dow Jones are all indexes of a limited number of stocks. Although they are useful tools for pegging where the market is they do not define the market as a whole. There are always opportunities to make money in stocks.

Next, we will move on to ETFs and mutual funds. These two securities are very similar in composition they just differ in how they are traded. Mutual funds and ETFs are made up of different stocks bundled together and many time they are made up of other funds to offer more diversification. These bundles are put together by a fund manager for a specific reason. Some may be geared toward asset appreciation while others may be put together for income production. With these funds, you should consider those with an investment objective that aligns with your goal.

    Another factor in selecting funds that are different than stocks is that funds have expense ratios. To put it in simple terms these fund managers have to make money and produce income to cover the fees that trade they make to create the funds, so they charge expense ratios to cover these fees. These fees are can be considered a sunk cost. They come out of what you put into the fund but you never actually see this transaction happen. It just cuts into your gains. So consider the expense ratio when you invest in funds. The

Donald Draper

ratio tends to be less than one percent although seeing funds with higher than one percent can happen. Actively managed mutual funds have a higher expense ratio than passively managed ones. Active management means the fund manager is actively changing the securities within the funds. Passive is the opposite, the fund manager is not active in the management of the fund, hence the lower expense ratio. ETFs, tend to passively manage so a majority of them have low expense ratios. Although expense ratios are a percentage based on what you invest they can become a large expense with a larger amount of money invested. Remember this when picking funds you get what you pay for. Although expense ratios are important, they shouldn't be the sole

Donald Draper

reason you select a fund.

There are different types of mutual funds and ETFs but there are two that I want to cover that are the more popular ones as of now. These are index funds and ETFs. Index funds are set up to mirror major indexes. The most popular are mirroring the S&P 500. You cannot buy directly into an index because they are not securities. But their movements are a barometer of the market as a whole. So along with the way, someone thought it would be a great idea to create funds made out of similar securities with an objective of following the indexes. Don't get me wrong, this isn't a bad strategy if you have a longer-term investment objective, twenty years or more. The market as a whole does show consistent growth over time. Index funds are highly popular when the index is on a tear and constantly showing large periods of growth. But the market and these indexes always goes through cycles and eventually have periods of shrinkage. When the indexes lose value these funds become less popular. So depending on your goals and time frame index funds may or may not be for you.

Next up are target date funds. These are funds that are specifically geared toward retirement. They have a specific date attached to them to represent a target retirement date. This date is important because it guides the fund manager to change the allocation of the fund to match the generic asset allocation of the people who buy these funds. Make a note that a person should never have more than one target date fund because they are made as a one fund solution. They are great for people who just want to put their money into something and forget about it for twenty years. That may work for some but the asset allocation is generic and may not work for more specific goals and time frames. Everyone is not the same.

The last thing to remember is the art of picking stocks and funds is developed through experience. The market moves in cycles so what works today may not work tomorrow. There are fortune 500 companies that have gone bankrupt. Luckily though with diversification, constant monitoring, and the ability to unemotionally make the buy and sell decisions, you will be able to manage your account yourself. This will save you money and should generally make you feel better about your financial life.

Donald Draper

How to Get Away With Money 96

Donald Draper

Chapter 11
What I leave you with

This book is a brief summary of all the knowledge and habits that I have gained over years of experience in the personal investing industry. Although this book isn't the end all be all for your own investing, it should be the foundation for you taking control of your investments.

I have seen it time and time again, I watched as investors who were being taken advantage of or wasting money just because they did not have a foundation to build on. Do not fall into the same traps as others. You know the tricks and have the knowledge to do this on your own. Investing, true personal

Donald Draper

investing is about being smart and patient. Not jumping on the current trends and having legitimate goals will lead to financial freedom. The ones who achieve their financial goals are the ones who save and make excellent financial decisions nine times out of ten and now you are on your way to being one of those who gets away with money.

There are many options for where you should put your money and decide to invest. To the average consumer, all these brokerages may seem to be all the same or very similar. They all have a website, offer online trading, have a 1-800 number etc. Those in the industry know the difference between firms

Donald Draper

and the specific ins and outs that make a great firm. Now that I am out of the industry I am going to share what I know about specific firms with you. Although you are now taking control of your own investments you still need to know where to put your money. There are some publications that will tell you who a great firm is and there are rating groups out there that give their opinion but they are influenced by outside factors and may not even know what's really going on. Through my career, I have worked with and have colleagues at these firms and I will break down which ones are the best and which ones to avoid by name. Where you choose to open your accounts and start your portfolio is just as important as what you invest in.

Donald Draper

-The BEST

Fidelity Investments, Charles Schwab, Td Ameritrade, Vanguard, T.Rowe Price

Pros: Not bank based and specialize in investments, great trading platforms, the self-directed side is great and has representatives that can help with securities. These representatives can explain a product to you whether it be a fund or a stock.

Cons: "service to sales" kings. They like everyone else are asset growth motivated. They will push those with assets over fifty thousand dollars into a managed product. Their sales techniques will make you doubt yourself if you do not fully believe you can manage your investments yourself.

-The Banks

Merrill Edge (Bank of America) Jp Morgan (Chase Bank) Capital One Investing

Pros: great websites, some have easy access to your cash, not product focused.

Cons: just looking for ways to bring in more money, usually a small business unit that the bank tends to not care about

-The Independents

Edward Jones, Morgan Stanley, LPL advisors, any other independent brokers

No Pros: they want to manage your money and charge outrageous fees.

Donald Draper

-The Insurance Agents

Northwestern Mutual, Mass Mutual, Penn Life, New York Life, AXA Advisors etc.

Life insurance is a great tool for the protection of assets and some tax-free income but it is not an investment. First of all these agents will call themselves financial advisors and most of them do not have the licenses to call themselves that. The agents that do will not specialize in investments. The small number that does specialize in investments are basically independent brokers that you should avoid. My advice is to use these guys for life insurance when you have the funds to spend on a whole life policy. Most employers offer a term life insurance policy that will cover your

Donald Draper

salary for one year if something were to happen to you.

-The Apps

Robin Hood, Betterment, Acorn

These apps offer low fees but lack the true stability that is only gained through being around for a long period of time. I suggest you always have access to someone to talk to you about a product. These apps may replace traditional brokerages in the future but right now I suggest not to using them. They haven't shown how they whether bad markets yet where people may act irrationally and take their assets out.

Some firms I want you to avoid at all cost. The ones that do not offer a

Donald Draper

self-managed option just avoid to save money. Independent advisors and insurance agents are just places that will take your money and fee you. Capital One investing by far has to be the worst self-directed options in the country. Their quotes are off and getting money in and out of the firm is a hassle. They are a small business unit of Capital One who themselves are just a credit card company that bought banks. Avoid at all costs. Merrill Edge is better but still just a small part of Bank of America and the little brother to Merrill Lynch (starting account balance $250k) Personally I believe that Fidelity is the best place to keep your investments although they will test you to acquire more of your money. They will say consolidation is key for simpler finances but

Donald Draper

investment money and personal money should be at separate places. If for some reason you do not want to go with Fidelity look into TD Ameritrade, Schwab, Vanguard, or T. Rowe

    Now get out there, open an account and get started. I guarantee someone or some company will try to tell you that you cannot manage your investments yourself but you know the tricks and you have got this. You will not fall into that trap or try to jump onto some penny stock bandwagon. You are educated and know how to get away with money.

Donald Draper

How to Get Away With Money 106

Donald Draper

Glossy of Investment Terms

- Ask price: the lowest price an owner is willing to accept
- Asset: Something that has the potential to earn money for you. Assets include stocks, bonds, commodities, real estate, and other investments.
- Asset allocation: One of the ways to divide up the holdings in your portfolio is to do so by asset class. The idea is that different assets perform opposite to each other, and you can limit some of your risks by allocating your portfolio according to the type of asset you have.
- Balance sheet: A statement showing what a company owns, as well as the liabilities the company has

Donald Draper

- Bear market: This is a market that is falling.
- Bid: This is the highest price a buyer is willing to pay when buying an investment.
- Blue chip: Blue chips are companies that have a long history of good earnings, good balance sheets, and even regularly increasing dividends.
- Bond: This is an investment that represents what an entity owes you.
- Book value: If you take all the liabilities a company has, and subtract them from the assets and common stock equity of the company, what you would have left over is the book value. Most of the time, the book value is used as part of an evaluative measure, rather than being truly related to a company's market value.

Donald Draper

- Broker: This is the entity that buys and sells investments on your behalf. Usually, you pay a fee for this service.
- Bull market: This is a market that is trending higher, likely to gain.
- Capital gain (or loss): This is the difference between what you bought an investment for and what you sell if for. If you buy 100 shares of a stock at $10 a share (spending $1,000) and sell your shares later for $25 a share ($2,500), you have a capital gain of $1,500. A loss occurs when you sell for less than you paid. So, if you sell this stock for $5 instead ($500), you have a capital loss of $500).
- Diversification: A portfolio characteristic that ensures you have more than one type of

asset. It also means choosing to buy investments in different sectors, industries, or geographic locations.
- Dividend: offer to divide up some of the income among shareholders. Dividends can be paid once or they can be paid more regularly, such as monthly, quarterly, semi-annually, or annually.
- Dow Jones Industrial Average: This average includes a price-weighted list of 30 blue chip stocks. Often used as a gauge of the health of the stock market as a whole
- Exchange: This is a place where investments, including stocks, bonds, commodities, and other assets are bought and sold.
- Index: A tool used to statistically measure

Donald Draper

the progress of a group of stocks that share characteristics.

- Margin: This is essentially borrowed money used to make an investment.
- Market capitalization: The market cap of a company is figured by multiplying its current share price by the number of shares outstanding.
- Over the counter (OTC stocks): Stocks that are not listed on any other the major exchanges. They tend to have lower prices and carry more risk
- NASDAQ: This is a stock exchange that focuses on trading the stocks of technology companies
- New York Stock Exchange: One of the most famous stock exchanges

- P/E (Price/ Earnings) ratio: This measure reflects how much you pay for each dollar that company earns. A company often reports profits on a per-share basis.
- Stock: A stock represents ownership in a company. Companies divide their ownership stakes into shares, and a number of shares you purchase indicate your level of ownership in the company. The stock is bought in the hopes that the company will be successful, and more people will want a stake, so you can sell your stake later at a higher price than you paid.
- Yield: This is associated with dividend investing and bonds. The yield represents the ratio between the stock price paid and

the dividend paid.

Donald Draper

www.ingramcontent.com/pod-product-compliance
Lightning Source LLC
Chambersburg PA
CBHW030846180526
45163CB00004B/1473